IS THAT CLEAR?

Effective communication
in a multilingual world

**Easy-to-follow tips for
adapting your English**

Zanne Gaynor & Kathryn Alevizos

For our dads who would have loved this book

Is That Clear?
Effective communication in a multilingual world

ISBN 978-1-9162800-0-7
eISBN 978-1-9162800-1-4

Published in 2019
© Zanne Gaynor & Kathryn Alevizos
www.acrobat-global.com

Design and production by Prepare to Publish Ltd
www.preparetopublish.com

Contents

Introduction

According to a report by the British Council,[1] non-native speakers of English now exceed the number of native speakers by an estimated ratio of 4:1 – and that number continues to grow.

If English is a global language, what's the problem?

The English that you, as a native speaker, use at home or with friends is unlikely to be the English that overseas associates have learned through more formal language training.

Problems in communication arise when there is no awareness of this difference.

---

[1] https://www.britishcouncil.org/sites/default/files/english-effect-report-v2.pdf

IS THAT CLEAR?

A 2015 survey of a NATO[2] working group looked at this very issue. The group consisted of around 30 members representing 25 countries. One of their findings was that

"...native speakers of English are not always good at adjusting their English to the manner and level that is used." [3]

Is this the right book for you?

Yes, if you're a native speaker of English and you work or socialise with people from other countries who don't speak English as their first language.

---

[2] North Atlantic Treaty Organization
[3] 'English as a lingua franca used at international meetings', Jana Barančicová & Jana Zerzová, Masaryk University, Czech Republic

Each chapter only takes a couple of minutes to read but offers invaluable advice that will reap long-term benefits.

Condensed into bite-sized chapters, *IS THAT CLEAR?* offers tips and strategies on how to adapt your language for more successful international communication. This handy reference tool is accessible and quick to read for the busiest of people.

In the book we use the following abbreviations:

E1: Refers to people who speak English as their first language or the language they feel most comfortable speaking.

E2: Refers to people who **don't** speak English as their first language. It may be their second, third, fourth language etc.

1.
Adapting your language

1.1 Time to pause

The first step to adapting your language is to slow down. You might start off speaking more slowly, but **once you get going, you often speed up** and this can lead to lack of clarity. Finding the right pace can be harder than it sounds especially if you want to **avoid unnatural and exaggerated language,** which includes speaking more loudly than you normally would.

So, what's the answer?

Adding pauses is a good way to **adjust the pace** of your language. If you listen to someone speaking Spanish, for example, it may seem like one continuous stream of sounds. You might not know where sentences start and finish, let alone words. This is also what English sounds like to E2 speakers.

By including pauses between sentences and ideas, you are breaking that continuous stream of sounds into manageable **bite-sized chunks of language**. This strategy helps E2 speakers to follow what you're saying.

Of course, it may feel forced at first, but it will have a positive effect on how you engage with E2 speakers.

 ACTION ITEMS

- Slow down but not too much.
- Adjust your pace by adding pauses.
- Avoid speaking in an unnaturally loud voice.

Cut down on unnecessary words

1.2

E1 speakers naturally fill gaps in speech with words or phrases such as:

...as it were...	...like/something like...
...sort of/kind of...	...well, basically...
...actually...	...I mean...
...y'know...	...literally...

These '**filler words**' are generally not a problem. However, they can make your **message unclear** to less proficient E2 speakers. Filler words add little or no meaning and make it harder for E2 speakers to unpick the main message.

Compare the two versions below.

Actually I'm not doing anything for my birthday, I mean most of my friends are basically working anyway.

I'm not doing anything for my birthday because my friends are working.

ACTION ITEMS

- Recognise what filler words you use – are they on the list mentioned in this chapter?

- Adjust your use of filler words according to the language level of E2 speakers.

- Avoid the temptation to fill every gap in the conversation – remember pauses are helpful.

1.3 Lost in translation

Everyday language that you think is simple can actually be quite complex for E2 speakers.

Take the sentence, 'She didn't *let on about* her new job.' For some E2 speakers, this is hard to understand as the **meaning** of *let on about* **isn't obvious**. The words can be **individually translated**, but **as a set, don't make sense**. In contrast, the sentence 'She didn't tell anyone about her new job' is far clearer.

Another reason why *let on about* is so difficult is that *let*, along with many other verbs (take, put, get etc.), **changes meaning depending on the word/words after** it. These are known as phrasal verbs or multi-word verbs.

He was *let out of* the meeting early. (allowed to leave)
The bad weather didn't show any signs of *letting up*. (stopping)

The **same combination** can even have **multiple meanings.**

He was *let off* with a warning. (released)
You can *let* me *off* here. (leave)

 ACTION ITEMS

- Be more aware of how much you use these word sets (phrasal verbs). Find alternative ways of saying the same thing.
- Look at Appendix A for some examples, e.g. set up = start.

1.4   At cross purposes

English is rich in **idiomatic phrases**. Although **idioms** give colour and interest to language, they are challenging for E2 speakers due to the fact that they often **make no sense when translated** and are often **culturally bound.**

Take the expression 'in a nutshell'. Most E2 speakers know what a nut and/or a shell is but they might not be familiar with the phrase. Even competent E2 speakers of English are likely to be baffled by certain idiomatic phrases.

Of course, to stop using idioms completely is unrealistic, but an **awareness** of how difficult they are to understand is **vital**.

ACTION ITEMS

- If using an idiom, try to paraphrase to make
  the meaning clear, for example,
  OK, let's <u>get the ball rolling</u>. Let's <u>start</u>.
  Shall we <u>call it a day</u>? Shall we <u>stop</u>?

- Look at the idioms in Appendix B. How many
  do you use on a regular basis?

1.5 Making small talk work

Many conversations begin and end with small talk – a comment on the weather or a sporting event. It helps put people at ease, doesn't it?

Sometimes, yes. But it is a minefield for E2 speakers who can find it **linguistically demanding and tiring**.

While the topics of small talk are simple, the **language is often idiomatic and vague**. Phrases such as '*Can't say I mind this hot weather!*' or '*The tennis had me on the edge of my seat*' are complex statements that can be difficult for E2 speakers to respond to. You might end up offering **lengthy explanations about throwaway comments** you only said to break the ice.

Added to this, topics covered in small talk can be **culturally specific**, leaving some E2 speakers unable to participate and feeling excluded.

 ACTION ITEMS

- Keep small talk simple and short and avoid overly colloquial language.
- Invite E2 speakers to join in, e.g. *Did you watch the tennis?*
- Try to refer to the E2 speaker's culture or interests, e.g. *Is tennis popular in your country?*

1.6 Questions can be difficult

Consider why the following examples are difficult:

You don't have time for a quick chat, do you?

I was wondering whether you might be able to spare a few minutes for a quick chat.

Both are more difficult to understand than you might think. The first begins with a negative structure '*You don't have...*' Until the '*do you*' is added at the end **it's unclear this is actually a question.** The E2 speaker has to mentally unravel this language.

The second is even more confusing as it's a very indirect way of asking a question. It begins with a past tense, '*I was wondering*', and that can be **misleading**. After all, it's about something that might happen in the future.

So, what's the solution?

Both questions could be replaced by 'Can we talk?' If you're worried it's too abrupt, using **the right tone** and adding the person's name will also help you to **sound polite.**

 ACTION ITEMS

- Avoid long, indirect questions. Use more direct question forms (Can you/Will you/Do you/Is there etc.).
- Allow time for the E2 speaker to answer your first question before asking more questions.

1.7 Disappearing sounds

In **natural conversation**, the **words** in a sentence **often merge**.

Do you want to go?   (D'ya wanna go?)
Will you get it later?   (Willya geddit later?)
I should have done it.   (I sh'ud've dunnit)

If an E2 speaker is struggling to understand you, it **may not be that your language is too difficult**. It could be that **words have merged, or individual sounds have disappeared**.

With time, E2 speakers will recognise this, but those who have limited experience with E1 speakers may find it more difficult.

ACTION ITEMS

- Avoid speaking mechanically but adjust your pace. As you slow down, the merging of words will reduce.

1.8 When politeness is a problem

We naturally use more polite speech to create a good first impression or to show respect. However, in an international setting, politeness **can be a barrier to communication.**

The notion of politeness is often **interpreted differently across cultures**. A direct style of speaking which is acceptable in one country could be interpreted as rude or even aggressive in another.

Linguistically, polite language is also tricky. It's often **indirect** and full of **unnecessary language** and **idioms**, e.g. *I'm afraid I don't think I'll be able to make it on Tuesday after all.* (I'm sorry, I can't come on Tuesday.)

Another issue that can be overlooked is that polite language can **hide** what **the real message** is. E.g., *'To be honest, I was a bit upset he arrived so late'* might be a polite way of saying I was really angry.

 ACTION ITEMS

- You might instinctively use polite language, but it can have a negative effect on the E2 speaker. Keep your language simple and your message clear.

- The lower the level of English that an E2 speaker has, the more direct their language will be. Don't interpret it as impoliteness.

2.
Inclusive not exclusive

2.1 Letting others join in

Ever felt like you **can't join in** a conversation? Maybe you missed the beginning or you just weren't ready. Perhaps you were a bit tired or weren't concentrating. It can happen to any of us – in our own language. Most of the time we find **a way of interrupting** or just **catching up**. It's all part of the natural flow of dialogue.

But when a person has to do that in a second or third language, it's more difficult and much more demanding.

Several factors can cause this; the **level** of English, the **topic** being discussed, the **speed** of the conversation or even the **number of speakers**.

E2 speakers sometimes find themselves **unable to formulate responses quickly enough**. The conversation has moved on before they've had the chance to contribute. This **passive role** can be frustrating for E2 speakers and may be **mistaken for lack of interest or opinion**.

 ACTION ITEMS

- Make an effort to include E2 speakers in conversations by using their name and asking simple, direct questions.
- Try to find one-to-one time with somebody who might be having difficulty joining in group conversations.

2.2 Making multilingual groups work

Groups work best when there is the right balance of skills and personalities. In international situations, **varying language abilities** can **affect a group's output**.

Optimal group dynamics come from a **good knowledge of the abilities** of people in that group, a **fair distribution of E1 speakers** amongst E2 speakers and a willingness to offer support where necessary. For example, in larger groups it's less daunting for an E2 speaker to check the meaning of something with a person nearby rather than asking the main speaker to stop or recap.

If there is **only one E1 speaker in the group**, be aware that that person needs to **move around** and **check** who might need support. Alternatively, get more competent E2 speakers to assist.

ACTION ITEMS

- Designate an E1 speaker as a 'go-to person' who can help E2 speakers with any queries.
- If possible, find out which E2 speakers may need support and team them up with more proficient speakers.

Does it all have to be in English?

2.3

No, not necessarily.

Offering the **opportunity** for E2 speakers to **use their own language** creates a **comfortable**, **more productive** and **fairer** environment. Allowing some time in a discussion for participants to discuss more complex issues in their own language can **generate additional ideas** and **useful feedback**.

By **including rather than excluding** other languages, E2 speakers have the chance to **express ideas or concepts** that they may have difficulty articulating in English.

Most E2 speakers don't just switch off their own language when they communicate in English. They might **process their ideas in their first language** before translating and transmitting them to others.

ACTION ITEMS

- Know who you're talking to. A questionnaire beforehand can reveal a person's preferred language.
- Allow E2 speakers to think about and discuss ideas in their own language and to feed back to the group in English.

2.4 Talks and presentations

The need for **clarity** in talks and presentations is even greater when the audience is made up of E2 speakers. Keeping **on topic** and **avoiding anecdotal or impromptu comments** is helpful.

As well as **adjusting the speed** of speech and **adding pauses**, it's important to **face the audience** as much as possible. A lot of communication is visual so being able to see **mouth and facial expressions** can aid understanding.

Avoid PowerPoints that require **a lot of reading** and **use visuals** when possible. If using written material, allow adequate time for E2 speakers to process the information before moving on. It will take them longer than E1 speakers. **Numbering sections** or **adding** clear **headings** will also help 'signpost' your presentation.

ACTION ITEMS

- Write numbers (dates, times etc) clearly on any slides or visuals. E2 speakers can easily mishear them.

- Explain acronyms/abbreviations the first time you use them. Don't assume they're common knowledge, eg ASAP, ETA etc.

- Allow time for breaks. Talks and presentations are tiring for E2 speakers and breaks offer a chance to clarify information.

2.5 Virtual conversations

Talking online is **especially challenging** for E2 speakers. As well as the familiar technical problems that can **delay** or **interrupt** the flow of a conversation and make effective participation difficult, the E2 speaker may experience **added complications**.

Poor sound quality makes it hard to pick up on the tone of a person's voice. If there is no video, the **lack of visual clues** restrict the ability to read a person's body language and may lead to **misunderstandings and confusion**.

In a group discussion, the conversation can be heavily **steered by the more assertive participants** (often E1 speakers) making it harder for others to join in.

ACTION ITEMS

- In a videoconference, agree how to interrupt or stop a conversation. Maybe a comment box on the side could allow participants to 'virtually' raise a hand.

- In group calls, get someone to keep an eye on the speed and difficulty of the call. Offer opportunities for clarification.

- Offer breaks if needed. Talking online is tiring.

3.
Last
but not
least

3.1 Identity crisis

Our use of language says a lot about us – where we come from, our **educational background** and even what **type of person we are** (confident, funny, calm etc.).

When speaking in another language this information is harder to transmit. Often E2 speakers find it **difficult to be the person that they are in their own language**. They can also feel their **professional status** is **undermined**. This is especially so when those with **less professional experience** but **better language** skills **dominate** the group discussion.

If this continues to occur, some **professionals** might eventually feel **excluded** and **choose to move** to a different working environment where their skills and ideas can be recognised, and their language skills accommodated.

! REMEMBER

- Speaking in a second language can affect your confidence and how your status is viewed.
- The people with the best ideas might not be the best communicators.

3.2 Pronunciation

Unlike many other languages, English is **not phonetic**. This means you can't always know how to pronounce a word by looking at how it's spelled.

Some words are also hard for E2 speakers to understand, or to pronounce, because of **silent letter**s e.g. ca*l*m, resi*g*n, ai*s*le, dou*b*t etc. **Place names** are also **notoriously difficult**. E2 speakers might expect Leicester to be pronounced *Lie-chester* and Norwich *Nor-witch*.

The **same letter or combination of letters** can be **pronounced in different ways**. The word *read*, for instance, is pronounced *red* or *reed* depending on context.

Consider the different ways that *ough* can be pronounced.

enough though bought drought cough through
Tricky, aren't they?

And what about the following?

He was too close to the door to close it.

! REMEMBER

- E2 speakers may recognise a word in written form, but not when they hear it. Writing down problematic words can help.

3.3 Accents

Around 350 million people speak English as their first language ... that's a lot of different 'Englishes'.

Words such as *glass* can be pronounced with a long or short vowel sound depending on which part of the UK the E1 speaker is from.

Likewise, E1 speakers from other parts of the world (USA, Canada etc.) have their own variations.

What does this mean for the E2 speaker?

Regional variations can be a shock for E2 speakers when they first encounter them. The majority of them may well have learned a more 'standard' version of English.

Many E2 speakers can adapt quickly but some may need some support initially.

❗ REMEMBER

- There is often a discrepancy between the standard English taught in many countries and all the regional or national variations of English spoken by E1 speakers.

- If you have a strong accent, pace your speech and resist using localised vocabulary and phrases.

3·4 Did you hear the one about...?

Sharing a joke can seem like a good way to defuse a difficult situation or just put people at ease. However, **in intercultural circles**, **humorous anecdotes** and remarks **can** often **fall flat**. Different cultures find different things funny.

Firstly, many jokes are a **play on words** or are **puns** and their **meaning** and **humour is lost** on the E2 speaker. Not getting the joke can lead to feelings of **embarrassment or exclusion** from the group.

Other humour may be in the form of **sarcasm** or **self-deprecatory comments** or even gently pulling someone's leg. Rather than seeing the funny side of this, E2 speakers might be confused or **see such comments** as **superficial** or **offensive**. Certain topics may even be **taboo** or **culturally inappropriate**.

! REMEMBER

- 'If in doubt, leave it out' is the best approach to using humour in an international setting.

Conclusion: is it time for change?

Yes, it is, if we want to become better international communicators.

But this requires a shift in mindset. Rather than relying on E2 speakers to raise their level of English to improve communication, we need to recognise the part we play. By implementing some of the strategies in this book, we can all make ourselves easier to understand.

The tricky thing is, our use of language is instinctive but we must challenge that instinct. For those of us with limited or no experience of learning a language or living and working abroad, this may be more demanding.

With the help of *IS THAT CLEAR?* we believe it's a skill that anyone can develop.

recognise

when your use of English is difficult for non-native speakers to understand

adapt

your English using a range of skills and strategies

communicate

more effectively in multilingual situations

Appendix A:
Phrasal verbs activity

The problem with phrasal verbs is that a change in preposition (with/to/at etc) can completely change the meaning.

Also, the phrasal verbs that E2 speakers learn may well be different to the ones that are commonly used by E1 speakers.

TASK 1:
What's the meaning of the phrasal verb in each of these sentences?

put away
Can you put those clothes away?
It's amazing how much bread he can put away.

put back
The strike put back the production by two months.
Can you put this back where you got it from?

IS THAT CLEAR?

put down
She's always putting her sister down.
Eric has put down £50,000 on a house.
My cat was put down at the weekend.
We usually put the baby down at about 7pm.

put off
Don't let me put you off the idea.
Turn the music down, it's putting me off!
The match has been put off because of the snow.

put on
Anna's very good at putting on accents.
We'll have to put on free transport on the night.

put out
Don't put yourself out, I'm happy to eat anything.
I really put my arm out playing tennis last night.
I felt put out when he rejected my idea.

TASK 2:
Put can be used with lots of other prepositions.

Take 5 minutes. How many sentences can you make with *put* and the following prepositions?

across   aside   by   forward   together

TASK 3:
Put is a phrasal verb than can also take two prepositions.

Make sentences with *put* and the following prepositions.

in for   down as   down for   down to   up with

IS THAT CLEAR?

TASK 4:
Look at the email. Can you think of ways to paraphrase the phrasal verbs in bold?

*Can't wait to ¹**catch up with** you! But first I've got to to ²**fill you in on** my plans for this summer. I've just ³**put down** a deposit on a camper van and I've ⁴**handed in** my notice! I've been thinking of ⁵**getting away** for a while and I've been ⁶**putting** some money **aside**. It wasn't hard ⁷**giving up** my job – you know I was fed up with that anyway. Anyway, let me know when you're free to ⁸ **meet up**!*

TASK 5:

A lot of everyday conversation includes more colloquial phrasal verbs that might not have been taught in English language courses.

Consider the different meanings of the verbs in the sentences. Compare what they 'literally" mean with what the speaker intends to say.

1 Let's **wrap up** early today.
2 Who wants to **kick off**?
3 He's difficult to **pin down**.
4 You should **kick back** and enjoy your freedom.
5 I really need to **brush up on** my French.
6 Don't **beat** yourself **up about** it.
7 I'm just going to **nip out for** a minute.
8 It'll **blow over**.
9 Could we **jazz up** the presentation a bit?
10 I'll **pop in** after work.

Appendix B:
Idioms activity

This is by no means an exhaustive list as there are thousands of idioms, but below is a list of some high frequency ones.

Look at the list and tick the ones you often use. Complete the gaps using your own words to explain the idioms.

IDIOMS	What they really mean
ahead of the game	*to be more successful than the competition*
at stake	*at risk*
back to square one	*to start something over again because a previous attempt failed*
back to the drawing board	*to start again and go back to the first stage of a project or process*

IS THAT CLEAR?

ballpark number/figure	*a very inexact estimate*
be in the dark	1 ...
between a rock and a hard place	*when there's no easy way out or good solution*
big picture	*everything that is involved with a particular situation*
blue sky thinking	*original or creative thinking to find a new solution or concept*
bottom line	*used to refer to the final outcome, or the most important point to consider*
by the book	*doing something strictly according to the rules, policies or the law*
call it a day	*when work has been completed for the day, or when you decide to stop working on an activity*
corner the market	*to dominate a particular market*

cut one's losses	*2 ...*
cut to the chase	*get to the most important point without wasting time*
cut-throat	*very intense, aggressive, and merciless competition*
game plan	*a strategy or plan for achieving success*
get something off the ground	*to start something (e.g. a project or a business)*
get the ball rolling	*to start something*
go down the drain	*your effort, work or money is wasted or lost*
go the extra mile	*to do more than what people expect*
hands are tied	*3 ...*
have your work cut out	*have something very difficult to do*
hit the nail on the head	*to do or say something 100% correctly*
in a nutshell	*using as few words as possible*

IS THAT CLEAR?

in full swing	*at a stage when the level of activity is at its highest*
it's not rocket science	*something is not complicated to understand*
jump the gun	*do something early or before the right time*
keep one's eye on the ball	*to give something one's full attention and to not lose focus*
learn the ropes	*learn the basics of something (e.g. a job)*
long shot	*something that has a very low probability of happening*
no strings attached	*something is given without involving special demands or limits*
no-brainer	*4 ...*
on a shoestring	*working on a tight budget or with very little money*
on the back burner	*low priority*

on the same page	*to be in agreement about something*
out in the open	*something that is public knowledge and not secret anymore*
out on a limb	*do or say something risky*
put all one's eggs in one basket	*to rely on only one thing to bring success*
put the cart before the horse	*to do or think about things in the wrong order*
raise the bar	*to set standards or expectations higher*
read between the lines	*understand what someone is implying or suggesting but not saying directly*
red tape	*official rules and processes that seem excessive and unnecessary*
rock the boat	*to do or say something that will upset people or cause problems*

IS THAT CLEAR?

run around in circles	*to keep doing something without achieving any real results.*
safe bet	*something that is certain to happen*
(be in the) same boat	5 ...
see eye to eye	*to agree with somebody*
see something through	*to continue until something is finished*
sever ties	*to end a relationship*
shoot yourself in the foot	*make things unnecessarily worse for yourself*
smooth sailing	*a situation where success is achieved without difficulties*
stand one's ground	*to not change one's opinion or position*
start from scratch	*to start again and go back to the first stage of a project or process*
stay on your toes	*to stay alert*

take the bull by the horns	*to directly confront a difficult situation in a brave and determined way*
the elephant in the room	*an obvious problem or controversial issue that no one wants to discuss*
the eleventh hour	*used to describe something that's done or happens at the last minute*
think outside the box	*to think of creative, unconventional solutions instead of common ones*
throw in the towel	*to quit*
throw the baby out with the bathwater	*6 ...*
touch base	*to make contact with someone*
twist someone's arm	*to convince someone to do something that he or she does not want to do*
up in the air	*something is undecided or uncertain*

IS THAT CLEAR?

up to speed
be familiar with current information

uphill battle
something that is difficult to achieve because of obstacles and difficulties

upper hand
to have more power than anyone else and so have control – have an advantage

word of mouth
something is given or done by people talking about something or telling people about something

Appendix C:
E2 speakers – issues and solutions activity

Having spent a lot of time in the classroom with E2 speakers, we have heard how difficult it can be to understand E1 speakers. Match the comment to the relevant chapter(s).

EG Comment 1: Chapter 1.7 Disappearing sounds

1: "I used to wonder why my teacher repeatedly used the word 'festival' at the start of lessons, it made no sense at all. When I asked her, I found out that what she had been saying was 'First of all…"

2: "The British and the Australians often sit near each other and stay together during the breaks. I guess they've got lots in common but I just can't follow their conversation or be part of it – especially if it's not on topic."

IS THAT CLEAR?

3: "I find it difficult to interrupt sometimes. Others just seem faster at doing that. I often play a more passive role, taking notes and try and address any queries at the end."

4: "I'm Spanish and sometimes struggle with my English. I usually try and sit next to somebody who is quite fluent. At least then, I can discreetly ask them to explain anything I don't understand."

5: "I'm usually a bit of a joker but suddenly I felt like I couldn't really share my humour with people. It left me feeling that others would see me as boring."

6: "I've always found videoconferencing the most stressful part of my job. Some calls last for hours and it's really tiring especially if they're late at night or early in the morning."

7: "Sometimes it's hard to follow what someone's saying, particularly if they're passionate about what they're talking about. I guess they just get carried away and assume we can all keep up."

8: "I asked my colleague if he wanted to go for a coffee. He gave me a very long answer, and never actually used the words yes or no, so I really wasn't sure what he wanted. In the end I had to ask if it was a yes or a no – it was a bit embarrassing."

Answer key

Appendix A – Phrasal verbs

Task 1

1 put in the correct place
2 eat
3 delayed
4 return
5 criticising
6 paid part of the total cost of something
7 humanely killed
8 put in bed
9 make you not like something
10 distracting
11 postponed
12 copying
13 provide
14 make a special effort / cause yourself more work
15 injured
16 felt upset or offended

IS THAT CLEAR?

Task 2
1 He finds it difficult to put his ideas across to the group.
2 We need to put aside our differences and move on.
3 Let's put some of that money by for our holiday.
4 I'll put my name forward for the new post.
5 We're putting together a list of things to do next week.

Task 3
1 She put in for a promotion but didn't get it.
2 I'd put that down as sheer incompetence.
3 I'm down for the match at the weekend, are you?
4 I put her poor exam result down to sheer exhaustion.
5 She puts up with his moods well.

Task 4
1 tell you my news
2 tell you
3 paid

4 given
5 travelling
6 saving
7 quitting
8 do something together

Task 5
1 Many E2 speakers will have learned *wrap* to mean put paper round a gift – nothing to do with finish.
2 This assumes a sporting knowledge – go first/start.
3 The word *pin* might be known as a tool/sewing accessory. It really means it's difficult to get a clear decision from him.
4 Again this will be recognised as a sport verb for most E2 speakers – nothing to do with relax.
5 *Brush* is a common word that will confuse E2 speakers in this context of to practise and improve.
6 E2 speakers might understand *beat* as to win or to hit but they might not get that it's actually to blame yourself.

IS THAT CLEAR?

7 The verb *nip* is difficult for E2 speakers as it isn't commonly found in coursebooks – 'out' helps them to guess but it isn't clear it means to go out quickly.

8 *Pass* may be understood in various ways, e.g. do well in an exam, move onwards but it isn't obvious it means become less difficult or go away.

9 Obviously *jazz* has musical connotations but here it means to make something more exciting.

10 *Pop* and *nip* are short and frequently used by native speakers but again it's not obvious to an E2 speaker that here it means to come and visit

Appendix B – Idioms

1 be uninformed
2 to stop doing something that is unproductive and won't ever generate results
3 not being free to behave in the way that you would like
4 something that is really obvious or easy
5 to be in the same difficult situation as someone else
6 eliminate or lose something good when trying to get rid of something bad

IS THAT CLEAR?

Appendix C – Comments from E2 speakers

1 This relates to Chapter 1.7, 'Disappearing sounds'. In this case, the three individual words (First/of/all) merged together in natural speech meaning that an easy phrase became unintelligible as the E2 speaker heard what they thought was a single word.

2 This could relate to either 1.5, 'Making small talk work', or 3.3, 'Did you hear the one about...?' In this case the E2 speaker finds the E1 speaker's conversation impenetrable. This may be because it covers culturally specific topics, such as British TV or local news items, or they could be sharing some 'in' jokes or indeed jumping from topic to topic rather than following one theme familiar to the E2 speaker.

3 This relates to Chapter 2.1, 'Letting others join in'. It raises the issue of how difficult it can be to interject in a conversation or discussion for E2 speakers. The problem may

not be in understanding the conversation but in the difficulty of formulating an appropriate response on the spot. By the time the E2 speaker is ready to join in, the conversation may have moved on to another point.

4 This relates to Chapter 2.2, 'Making international groups work'. The E2 speaker in this case is aware of how teaming up with a more competent E2 speaker can support them. Not all E2 speakers may be aware of the benefits of this so it's a good idea to suggest these kinds of pairings.

5 This relates to Chapter 3.1, 'Identity crisis'. Feelings of frustration and a loss of 'the self' are frequently experienced by E2 speakers and often overlooked by the E1 speaker. Be aware of this and acknowledge it where possible. Your international colleagues will appreciate it.

6 This relates to Chapter 2.5, 'Virtual conversations'. It highlights the issues regarding videoconferencing for E2 speakers. This particular person could be helped by having a clear written agenda in advance so that they can anticipate the topics to be discussed, and feel more prepared. Also, finding times that suit all parties and incorporating regular breaks during the course of a videoconference can help.

7 This could relate to Chapter 1.1, 'Time to pause', and 1.2, 'Cut down on unnecessary language'. It raises the problem faced by E2 speakers when E1 speakers talk too fast and don't break up their speech into smaller chunks by pausing between points. It can also be a result of E1 speakers using too much filler language (sort of/basically/kind of etc.).

8 This relates to Chapter 1.8, 'When politeness is a problem'. In trying to politely decline an offer, the E1 speaker has unintentionally,

created an awkward situation for the E2 speaker. The E1 speaker may have replied to the offer of coffee with something such as, 'thanks, I'd love to but I've already had a couple today and I'll be buzzing if I have another one'. Look at the beginning of the answer 'thanks, I'd love to'... it could sound like a yes if the rest isn't understood.

About the authors

Zanne Gaynor has taught business English in companies such as Gillette and Banco Hipotecario in Spain as well as general English in schools in Germany and the UK. She has also been a translator for an international photographic company.

Between 2003 and 2006, Zanne set up and ran her own government-accredited language school in the Balearic Islands. Her books have been published by Pearson, Macmillan and Richmond and she has written English language exams for Trinity.

Zanne now lives in Oxfordshire, where she has recently worked as a volunteer with asylum seekers. In June 2019 she graduated from Oxford Brookes with a postgraduate award in Education (TESOL). Zanne speaks French, German and Spanish.

IS THAT CLEAR?

Kathryn Alevizos has lived and worked in France and Greece. On returning to the UK, she taught business English to companies including BMW and Schlumberger as well as teaching general English in universities and private language schools. She also spent several years teaching refugees and asylum seekers in colleges of further education. She has worked as a teacher trainer on CELTA courses and is a published author with Pearson. Kathryn is a consultant for Cambridge Assessment and has chaired and written for various international exams.

Kathryn now lives in Gloucestershire with her Greek husband and two children. Having a second language in her family has given her an added insight into the challenges of international communication.

Their story

As language graduates Zanne and Kathryn have always had an interest in international communication. They met while co-authoring a course book for Pearson Education. Having created materials to support E2 speakers, they felt that more support should be offered to E1 speakers working or socialising in multilingual settings. This was when they first had the idea for *IS THAT CLEAR?*. If you'd like to learn more about them and what they do, join them on their website **www.acrobat-global.com**

Acknowledgements

A huge thanks to a wonderful group of people who have given us invaluable support and feedback during the writing of this book. They were all an integral part in turning our idea into reality: Nicole Ashbrook, Jana Barančicová, Carolyn Barraclough, Patricia Bartley, Geoff Barton, Debbie Birch, Penny Campbell, Lisa Collet, Tina Ewens, Paul Gaynor, Paul Harris, Viv Lambert, Clare Lucas, Dr Anthony Manning, Siobhan McGuire, Rita Mistry, Grahame Newton, Robert Scott, Tim Walker, Jana Zerzová.

Thanks also to Andrew Chapman who brought our ideas to life with his clear-sighted suggestions and excellent editorial and design services.

IS THAT CLEAR?

Of course, we couldn't have done it without the love and patience of our families; Zanne's husband David and their children, Rose, Thomas and George, and Kathryn's husband Dimitris and their children, Eleni and Sophia. A couple of pets played their part too!

And finally, a special thanks to two very important women in our lives – Zanne's mother-in-law Eileen Walker and Kathryn's mum Margaret Hammond. A constant source of positive energy.

Lightning Source UK Ltd.
Milton Keynes UK
UKHW050444211222
414149UK00013B/174